# take-along totes

## Mix & Match Your Way to Creative Organization

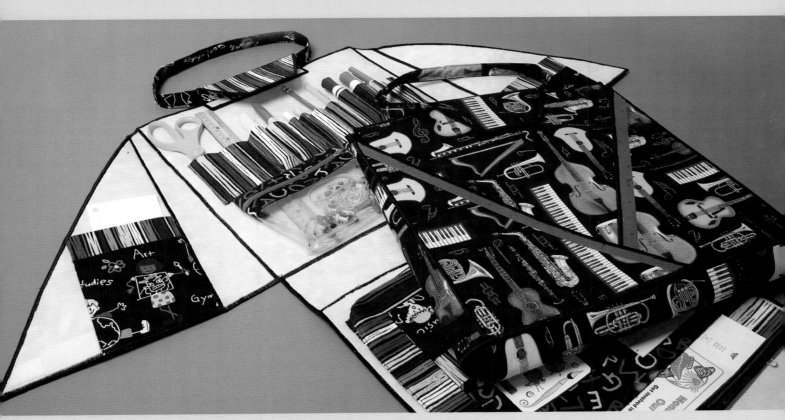

## MARILYNN BILYEU

C&T PUBLISHING

Text copyright © 2008 by Marilynn Bilyeu

Artwork copyright © 2008 by C&T Publishing, Inc.

Publisher: Amy Marson

Editorial Director: Gailen Runge

Editor: Stacy Chamness

Technical Editors: Carolyn Aune and Jane Miller

Copyeditor/Proofreader: Wordfirm Inc.

Design Director/Cover & Book Designer: Christina D. Jarumay

Production Coordinator: Kirstie L. Pettersen

Illustrator: John Heisch

Photography by C&T Publishing, Inc., unless otherwise noted

Published by C&T Publishing, Inc., P.O. Box 1456, Lafayette, CA 94549

Library of Congress Cataloging-in-Publication Data

Bilyeu, Marilynn.

   Take-along totes : mix & match your way to creative organiza-
tion / Marilynn Bilyeu.

      p. cm.

   ISBN 978-1-57120-450-9 (pbk. : alk. paper)

   1. Tote bags.  I. Title.

   TT667.B55 2007

   745.594—dc22

                                        2007025102

Printed in china

10 9 8 7 6 5 4 3 2 1

# dedication

*This book is dedicated to my best friend and husband, Richard, who gives me encouragement and support in all of my endeavors; makes homemade vegetable soup, spinach salads, and other delectable foods to nourish me; and reminds me that I should stop and eat, take a walk in the woods, or just relax once in a while. Without him I would probably just sew and eat chocolate nonstop.*

# acknowledgments

Thanks so much to my sewing and shopping buddy, sister, and dearest friend, Nancy Hill, for all of her help testing my patterns, sharing ideas, working on models, and just being there.

A special thank you to my daughters, Suzanne and Krista; my granddaughter, Ericka; my sister-in-law, Connie; my nieces, Gay Lea and Carol; and my bridge group friends for sharing their innovative ideas for *Take-Along Totes*.

Thanks to Darlene Christopherson for suggesting that I contact C&T Publishing.

Thanks to Judy, Carlene, and others in our guild for your encouragement.

Without my fun-loving editor, Stacy, and my techi-precise editor, Carolyn, this book would not have been nearly as enjoyable to do. Thanks for keeping me laughing and on track.

A special thanks to the following companies for their generosity in supplying fabrics, threads, and other products used for the projects in this book: Andover Fabrics, C&T Publishing, Clothworks, Kandi Corp, Lion Brand Yarn, Michael Miller Fabrics, P&B Textiles, Timeless Treasures, 2 Point Media, Wrights Sewing Products, and YLI Corporation.

# contents

 # introduction

For as long as I can remember, I have loved to sew. My mom made most of our clothes when I was a child and, being the last of three girls in line for the hand-me-downs, that wasn't too exciting for me. My grandmother piqued my interest in sewing, however, when she made clothes for my Ginny Doll one Christmas. By the next year, first on my wish list was a sewing machine. Santa came through with a little Singer model for children that had a hand crank and made a chain stitch. With all the scraps I could possibly need, I was in seventh heaven. Of course, I had no patterns, but who needed them when you had a model like Ginny, who didn't have many curves to her figure and for whom you could make a gathered skirt out of a rectangle?

Since joining the quilting world, I needed a way to store my appliqué supplies so they were easy to take along when I visited my mom at the nursing home, went on a trip or to a quilt meeting, or just sat in my favorite chair for an evening of stitching. I couldn't find what I wanted anywhere, so I reverted back to my Ginny Doll days and made up my own pattern, which I'm looking forward to sharing with you.

Create a tote designed to fit your specific needs or make a personalized gift that is sure to be a hit. Instructions are included for a Take-Along Tote for Quilters, with adaptations for scrapbookers, knitters, teachers, girls on-the-go, and kids on-the-go. Or combine and adapt the patterns for endless possibilities!

# planning your tote

## Before You Begin

Take some time to look through this book. Choose a design that is featured in the book or customize the pockets and accessories to meet your needs (page 41). After making your decisions, read through the entire pattern for the tote, pockets, and accessories that you have chosen. If you are using a panel fabric or a one-way design, study the pattern to determine which portion of the fabric will end up on the front before you cut the fabrics for the pockets and accessories. Change the size of a pocket to fit the design on the fabric or sew borders onto a piece of fabric to enlarge it to the right size. The more you let the fabrics work for you, the more fun you will have making your tote. Allow yourself plenty of time, take lots of chocolate breaks, and have fun!

## Choosing the Fabric

Choosing a fabric is my favorite part of any project. The simplest method for this project is to find a collection that you love and go from there. Try to find a collection with a fairly large-scale motif for the main theme fabric. Then use the coordinating fabrics for the pockets and accessories. Panels also work very nicely.

*Under the Big Top* collection by P&B Textiles

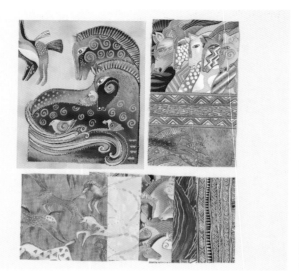

*Mythical Horses* **collection by Laurel Burch for Clothworks**

Using a collection takes out some of the guesswork, because you *know* the fabrics will look good together. It then becomes a simple matter of choosing which fabric to use where.

*Willowberry Winter* **by Maywood**

*Renaissance* **by P&B Textiles**

If you can't find a collection that suits you, choose a theme fabric for the exterior and find coordinating fabrics for the interior and the accessories. Look for stripes for the divided pockets and motifs to fussy cut for accessories.

*Carnival Bloom* **collection by Michael Miller Fabrics**

**Fabrics from** *Timeless Treasures* **by Dan Norris and Andover Fabrics, and The Gail Kessler/Ladyfinger Studio**

Choose a good-quality fabric so that your tote will hold up well. Home decor fabrics work well for the exterior, but the accessories will be easier to make with lightweight 100% cotton.

Another idea is to use an orphan quilt block to set the theme for your tote. Leftover scraps from a block may be enough for use on pockets or accessories. Feature embroidered fabrics on the back of the tote and add touches of embroidery to the flaps, pockets, and accessories. Decorative stitching looks nice on the pocket tops. Use your imagination and have fun!

# Threads

Any good-quality, machine-embroidery thread will work for the satin stitching on this project. Be sure to do some trial sewing on scraps to determine which threads work best with your fabric and your machine.

# Tools

- Basic sewing supplies
- Sewing machine with a zigzag stitch
- Sharp machine needles (size 70/10 or 75/11)
- Topstitch machine needles (size 80/12)
- Appliqué foot or open-toe foot for your sewing machine
- ¼" foot (not a must, but you'll love it for piecing)
- Narrow-edge or topstitch foot (great for connecting pieces, although an appliqué foot will work, too)
- Teflon foot (not a must, but can ease the making of the vinyl pouches)
- Rotary cutter
- Cutting mat and rulers
- Markers that you trust will wash off (I prefer the white iron-off type or a sliver of soap.)
- Iron and ironing surface
- Teflon pressing sheet
- Temporary adhesive spray (not a must, but it helps)

# Supplies

- Fabric A 1 yard for all exterior pieces, the handle, and the bottom pocket on the 7-pocket unit
- Fabric B 1 yard for lining all pieces
- Fabric C 1 yard for the accordion pouch and various pockets
- Fabric D 3 or 4 fat quarters or large scraps of coordinating fabrics for various pockets and accessories

- Pellon Craft Fuse or Decor-Bond or similar iron-on backing ½ yard for accordion pouch
- fast2fuse Double-Sided Fusible Stiff Interfacing 1 yard
- ⅛" thick heavy stabilizer 1½ yards (Skip if using fast2fuse.)
- Fusible web 2½ yards (Skip if using fast2fuse.)
- Batting for tote handle

  1 piece ¾" × 25", except for Girls-on-the-Go Tote

  **Girls-on-the-Go Tote:** 1 piece ¾" × 36"
- Thread

  Coordinating thread for construction

  Machine embroidery thread for satin stitching

  Invisible thread for stitching the vinyl pouches and the hook-and-loop tape
- Quilter's Vinyl or other clear vinyl ⅜ yard for the removable pouches (See Sources, page 47.)
- ¾"- or ⅝"-wide sew-in hook-and-loop tape ⅝ yard for the vinyl pouches and tote closures
- ¼"-wide elastic 1 yard for thread holder (Quilter's Tote); ¼ yard for the large division in the tool pocket (Tote for Music Teachers and Kids-on-the-Go Tote)
- 7"–9" polyester zippers 2 for the vinyl pouches (Only one is needed for the Quilter's Tote. One of the zippers must be 9" for the Girls-on-the-Go Tote.)
- *Optional: 4½ yards of ¹⁄₁₆" polyester cording (only comes in white) or size 3 Coats & Clark Fashion Crochet Thread (match the color of the exterior of the tote as close as possible)*
- ***Additional Suppies For the Quilter's Tote:***

  Felt 2" × 7¼"

  Template plastic 2 pieces 3¾" × 2¼"

  Fiberfill a small amount

> **Tip**
>
> Although using fast2fuse will save several steps, you could also add fusible to both sides of heavy ⅛" stabilizer. Fusible made for machine stitching won't gum up your needle.

# beginning steps

## CUTTING

*The width is listed first.*

> **NOTE:** *Copy parts A and B of Pattern Pieces 1 and 3 (pages 12–13). Join the parts before cutting the pieces listed below.*

### Fabric A

- 2 pieces 15″ × 15″ for front and back

- 3 pieces 3¾″ × 15″ for the bottom and sides

- 2 front flaps—Pattern Piece 1 (cut one right side up and one wrong side up)

> **NOTE:** *If you add a coordinating decorative strip of fabric to the flap, cut the strip ¼″ wider than the finished strip width plus another ¼″ for the amount that will be lost when the flap is trimmed. Stitch the strip to the cut flap using a ¼″ seam and press toward the decorative strip prior to fusing.*

- 1 piece 2¼″ × 25″ for the handle, *except for the Girls-on-the-Go Tote* (see page 12)

- 1 piece 10½″ × 8½″ for the bottom pocket on the 7-pocket unit

### Scrapbooker's Tote

- 1 piece 2¾″ × 20″ for the ruler pocket

### Fabric B for lining

- 2 pieces 15″ × 15″ for front and back

- 3 pieces 3½″ × 15″ for bottom and sides

- 2 front flaps—Pattern Piece 1 (cut one right side up and one wrong side up)

- 1 piece 7½″ × 6½″ for the top closure lining

### Fabric C

- 1 piece 18½″ × 28½″ for the accordion pouch

### Fabric A, B, C, or D

- 1 piece 6¼″ × 9″ for the left inside flap pocket

- 1 piece 5¼″ × 13″ for the right inside flap pocket

- 1 piece 20″ × 8″ for the tool pocket, *except for Knitter's Tote and Girls-on-the-Go Tote*

- 1 piece 7½″ × 6½″ for the top closure

- 1 piece 10½″ × 16½″ for the large top pocket of the 7-pocket unit

- 2 pieces 10½" × 8½" for the second and third small pockets of the 7-pocket unit

- 1 piece 4" × 5" for the accordion pouch closure tab

- 4 strips 3" × 7" for the zippers on the vinyl pouches, *except for Quilter's Tote and Girls-on-the-Go Tote*

### Knitter's Tote

- *1 piece 8" × 8" for the tool pocket*

- *2 pieces 6" × 19" for the needle pockets*

### Girls-on-the-Go Tote

- *1 piece 20" × 7" for the tool pocket*

- *1 piece 2¼" × 36" for the handle*

- *2 strips 3" × 5½" and 2 strips 3" × 9" for the vinyl pouches*

### Quilter's Tote

- *2 strips 3" × 5½" for the vinyl pouch*

- *1 piece 4" × 9½" for the pincushion* (If fussy cutting fabric for the Quilter's Tote pincushion, see Tip on page 22 for measuring and cutting to fit your fabric image.)

- *1 piece 3" × 8¾" for the needle case*

- *1 piece 3" × 8¾" for the needle case lining*

Label each cut piece of fabric, stabilizer, and fusible, then mark them with an arrow pointing to the top.

### Pellon Craft Fuse or Decor-Bond or other similar iron-on backing 1 piece 13" × 11½"

### Quilter's Vinyl

- 2 pieces 7" × 4½" and 2 pieces 7" × 6½" for the vinyl pouches, *except for the Quilter's Tote and the Girls-on-the-Go Tote*

- *For Quilter's Tote: 1 piece 5½" × 3½" and 1 piece 5½" × 5½"*

- *For Girls-on-the-Go Tote: 1 piece 5½" × 3½" and 1 piece 5½" × 5½"; 1 piece 9" × 4½" and 1 piece 9" × 6½"*

### fast2fuse

- 2 pieces 14½" × 14½"

- 3 pieces 3" × 14½"

- 1 piece 7¼" × 6¼" for the top closure

- 2 front flaps using Pattern Piece 1

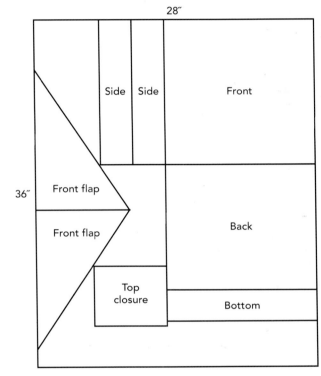

Layout on fast2fuse.

*If you're using fast2fuse, the stabilizer and web are not necessary.*

### Nonfusible stabilizer

- 2 pieces 15" × 15"

- 3 pieces 3½" × 15"

- 1 piece 7½" × 6½" for the top closure

- 2 front flaps using Pattern Piece 1

### Fusible web

- 4 pieces 14½" × 14½"

- 6 pieces 3¼" × 14½"

- 2 pieces 7" × 6" for the top closure

- 4 front flaps using Pattern Piece 1

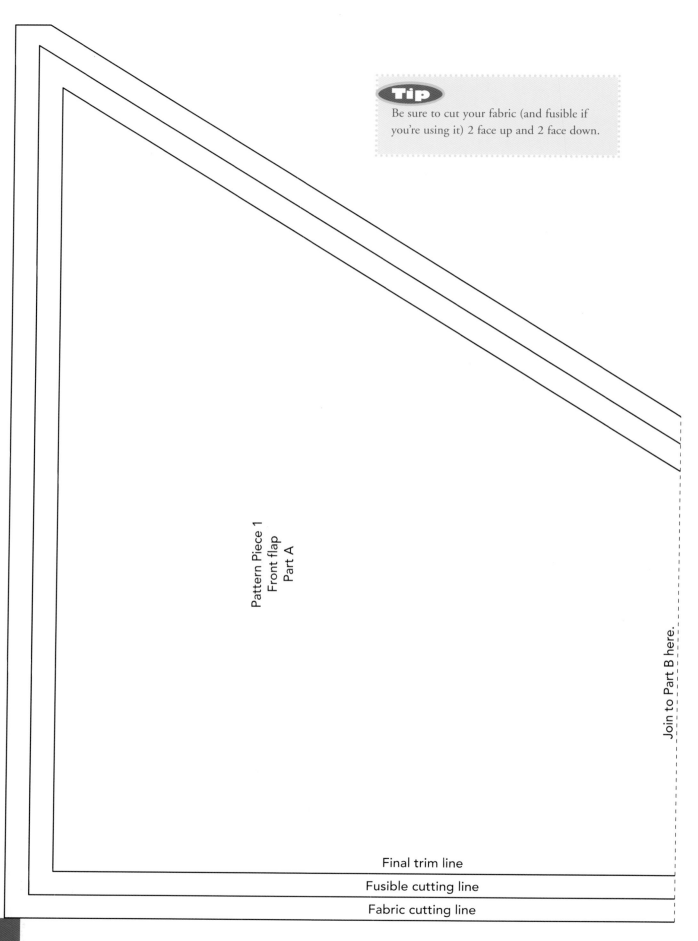

**Tip**

Be sure to cut your fabric (and fusible if you're using it) 2 face up and 2 face down.

Pattern Piece 1
Front flap
Part A

Join to Part B here.

Final trim line

Fusible cutting line

Fabric cutting line

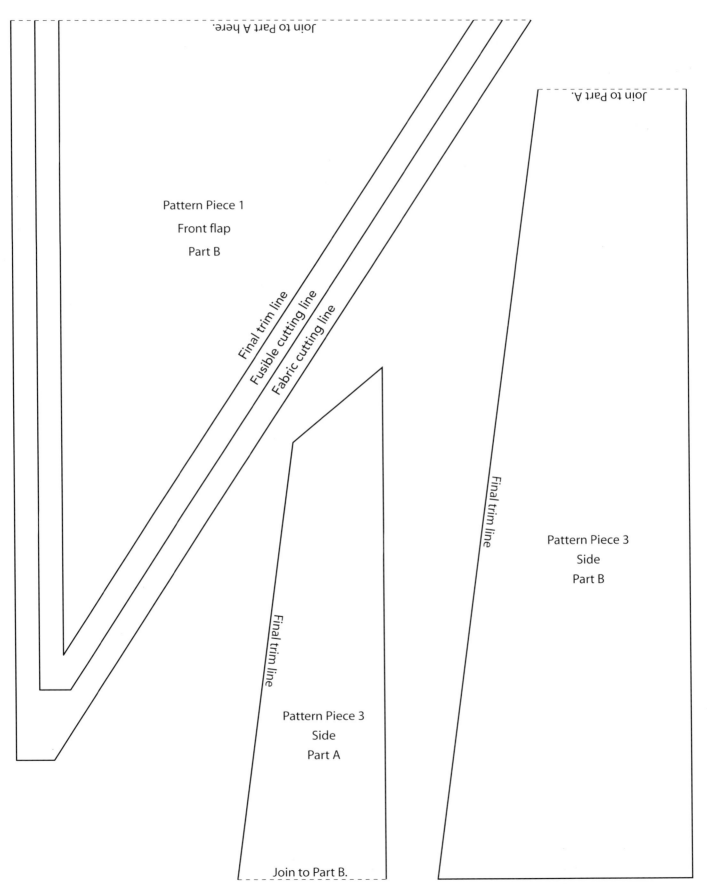

Join to Part A here.

Join to Part A.

Pattern Piece 1

Front flap

Part B

Final trim line

Fusible cutting line

Fabric cutting line

Final trim line

Pattern Piece 3

Side

Part B

Final trim line

Pattern Piece 3

Side

Part A

Join to Part B.

Sides

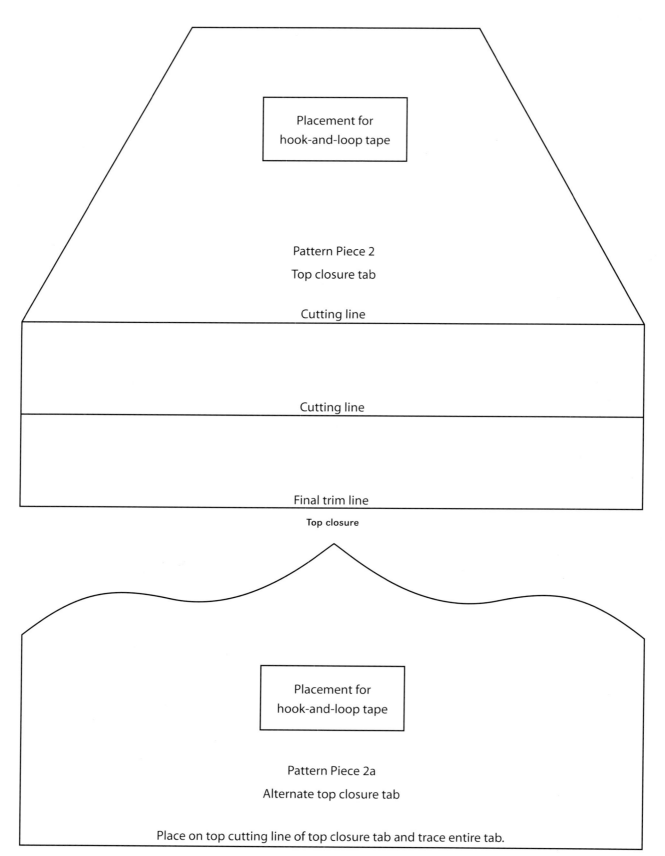

Placement for
hook-and-loop tape

Pattern Piece 2

Top closure tab

Cutting line

Cutting line

Final trim line

**Top closure**

Placement for
hook-and-loop tape

Pattern Piece 2a

Alternate top closure tab

Place on top cutting line of top closure tab and trace entire tab.

**Top closure, alternative option**

## FUSING THE LINING

*I recommend using a Teflon pressing sheet.*

**1.** **If using fast2fuse, go to Step 2.** Apply fusible web to only one side of each piece of stabilizer. Center the pieces so that the edges of the fusible are about ¼" inside the edges of the stabilizer.

**2.** Following the manufacturer's directions, fuse the lining fabrics to the fast2fuse or other stabilizer front, back, sides, bottom, side flaps, and top closure pieces, being sure to center them so the stabilizer is about ¼" inside the edges of the fabric. Do not trim the edges yet.

## TOP CLOSURE

Mark the cutting and placement lines for Top Closure Pattern Piece 2 or 2a (page 14) on the lining side of the top closure 7½" × 6½" piece. Stitch a 1½" piece of hook-and-loop tape (stiff side) as marked. Do not trim the shapes yet.

## INSIDE FRONT FLAP POCKETS

**Interior of flap pockets with hook-and-loop tape in place**

**1.** Fold the pockets in half, wrong sides together, to measure 6¼" × 4½" for Pocket 1 (left inside flap) and 5¼" × 6½" for Pocket 2 (right inside flap). Press. The fold is at the top of the pocket.

If your fabric has a one-way design, check to be sure it is facing properly.

**2.** Turn the pockets right sides together, with the desired pattern for the front of the pocket facing down, or on the underside. With the fold at the top, stitch the left side seam of Pocket 1 and the right side seam of Pocket 2 with a ¼" seam. Trim the corner, turn, and press.

**3.** Topstitch across each pocket ½" down from the top folded edge.

**4.** Sew Pocket 1 to the lining side of the left flap. With the pocket facing up, align the unfinished pocket edges with the vertical sides and the bottom of the flap. Use a ⅝" seam to baste along the unfinished edges. Sew Pocket 2 on the lining side of the right flap in the same manner.

**5.** Edgestitch along the finished side of each pocket.

**6.** On the lining side of the left flap, sew a 2" piece of hook-and-loop tape (stiff side) ⅝" up from the bottom edge and butted against the pocket.

**7.** On the lining side of the right flap, sew a 2" piece of hook-and-loop tape (stiff side) ⅝" up from the bottom edge, beginning at the pointed edge of the flap. Trim the hook-and-loop tape to fit the flap.

## POUCH POCKET WITH 7-POCKET UNIT

**Large pouch pocket with attached 7-pocket unit**

**1.** Fold the 18½" × 28½" piece of fabric for the pouch in half, wrong sides together, to measure 18½" × 14¼". Press. The fold will be at the top of the pocket. If your fabric has a one-way design, be sure it is oriented correctly.

**2.** With the front of the pouch on top, open the folded fabric piece and position the 13″ × 11½″ piece of Pellon Craft Fuse on the wrong side of the bottom half of the fabric. The 13″ edge of the Craft Fuse should be against the fold line, with equal amounts of fabric on either side. Fuse according to the manufacturer's directions.

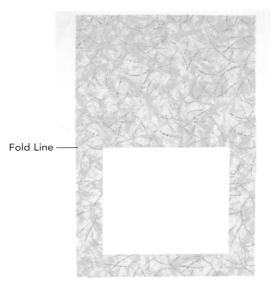

Fold Line —

**Wrong side up**

**3.** Fold the pouch fabric in half with right sides together. Stitch with a ¼″ seam allowance along the sides and the bottom.

**4.** With the folded edge at the top, mark a 2¾″ × 2¾″ square at each bottom corner. Cut out the squares.

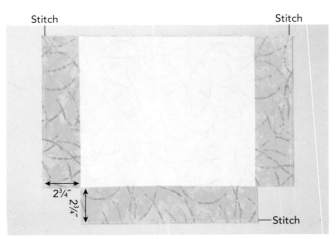

Stitch | Stitch

2¾″

2¾″

—Stitch

**Wrong side of pouch pocket with Craft Fuse attached and corners removed**

**5.** Turn the pouch right side out through one of the cut corners and press. Topstitch 1″ down from the fold at the top edge of the pouch.

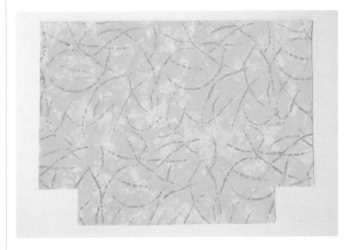

**6.** Fold the side flaps toward the center of the inside of the pouch, creating a fold right along the edge of the Craft Fuse. Edgestitch along each *folded* edge. Press the flaps toward the outside of the pouch. Repeat this step with the bottom flap.

**Edgestitch along pouch's folded edge.**

**7.** Create a permanent crease for the accordion folds in the pouch pocket: With the right side of the pouch facing up, fold up each flap so that it just meets the stitching. Press and edgestitch along the folded edge of each flap.

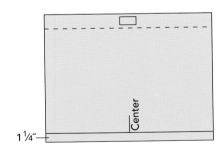

Edgestitch along the accordion folds.

**8.** Center a 1″ piece of hook-and-loop tape (stiff side) along the top edge of the pouch pocket above the topstitching. Stitch into place.

**9.** Mark the placement of the 7-pocket unit by marking a line across the bottom of the pouch front 1¼″ up from the edgestitching. Make a small mark just above the line at the center of the pouch. Set this piece aside.

Mark the pouch for placing the 7-pocket unit.

**10.** Fold the fabric for the largest pocket of the 7-pocket unit in half, wrong sides together, to measure 10½″ × 8¼″. Press to create the fold at the top of the pocket.

**11.** Mark the largest pocket of the 7-pocket unit to determine placement of the smaller pockets. With the folded edge at the top, mark a line across the front of the pocket 1″ up from the bottom edge. Mark another line 1″ above the first.

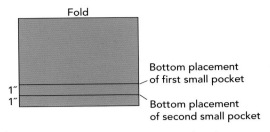

Mark the pouch pocket for the smaller pocket placement.

**12.** Fold each piece for the small pockets in half lengthwise, wrong sides together, to measure 10½″ × 4¼″.

**13.** Topstitch across the top of each small pocket ½″ down from the fold. Leave the bottom open.

**14. Attach the small pockets to the large pocket.** Open the large pocket flat, right side up. Place a small pocket face up with the bottom of the pocket aligned with the top marked line. Stitch, using a ¼″ seam, along the unfinished bottom edge of the small pocket. Place the bottom of the second small pocket at the lower marked line and stitch along the unfinished bottom edge. Place the last small pocket at the bottom edge of the large pocket. Stitch along the unfinished bottom edge using a ¼″ seam.

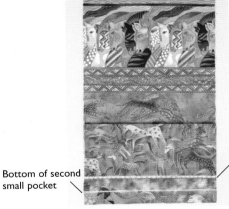

**15.** Fold the large pocket in half, right sides together with the small pockets in place and the fold at the top. Trim the edges even, if necessary. Stitch down each side, using a ¼″ seam. Turn right side out and press.

**16.** Topstitch ½″ down from the folded edge along the top of the large pocket.

**17.** Fold the pocket unit in half, side edges together, and press to form a crease. Open the pocket. Topstitch on the creased line, starting at the bottom edge and ending at the top of the last small pocket. Stitch again on top of the first stitching line to reinforce it.

**18. Attach the 7-pocket unit to the accordion-folded pouch pocket.** Place the 7-pocket unit wrong side up, with the raw edge of the unit along the bottom line marked on the pouch pocket. The top of the pocket unit will be upside down below the line. Match the center of the pocket with the marked center of the pouch and pin in place. Stitch along the raw edge of the pocket using a ¼" seam allowance.

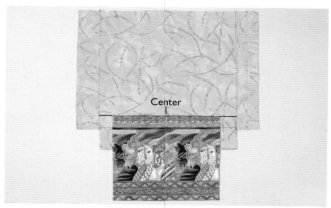

7-pocket unit face down, with the bottom of the unit at the top and stitched across the bottom

**19.** Flip the pocket into position and press.

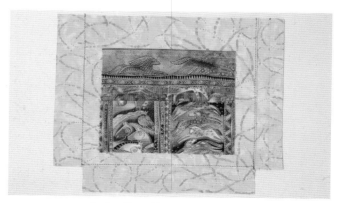

Pocket flipped into place on pouch

**20.** Edgestitch each side of the pocket unit from top to bottom. Edgestitch along the bottom edge. Secure all stitching lines with backstitching.

**21. Attach the pouch.** With right sides together, fold the edges of the cutout corners to meet. Align the outer edge of the bottom flap with the outer edge of the adjacent side flap. This will create a 45° fold in the pouch. Start at the inside corner of the flaps and stitch along the raw edge using a ¼" seam allowance. Stop ¼" before the end and backstitch, leaving the last ¼" open. Repeat on the other corner.

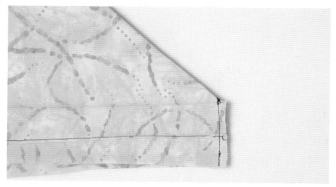

Stitch the bottom corner.

**22.** Fold each flap accordion style and manipulate the corners to lie flat. Press.

Corners should look like this.

**23.** Mark a line across the tote front lining 2″ down from the top edge. Mark another line 1½″ up from the bottom edge. Mark a vertical line 1″ in from the edge on each side. Mark another line 1½″ down from the top center for the tab closure.

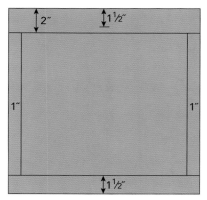

Mark for pouch placement.

**24.** Position the pouch on the tote front lining, right side up and with the top of the pouch aligned with the top marked line on the tote. The bottom and side pouch edges should meet the lines on the side and bottom tote edges. Edgestitch from top to bottom on each side of the pouch, making sure the accordion folds do not get caught in the stitching. Then edgestitch along the bottom edge of the pouch.

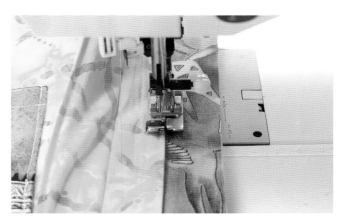

Stitch the pouch onto the tote front lining.

**25.** **Create the pouch closure tab.** Fold the 5″ × 4″ piece of fabric in half, wrong sides together, to measure 2½″ × 4″. Press to form a crease. Open the strip and fold the outer edges to meet at the centerline (just like making bias tape). Press closed.

Fold the tab closure as you would fold bias tape.

**26.** Open at the center fold line (keeping the outer edges folded). Fold the right sides together at the center fold. Sew across each end with a ¼″ seam allowance. Trim the corners. Turn and press. Topstitch along all edges.

**27.** Sew a 1″ piece of hook-and-loop tape (soft side) to the underneath side of one end of the tab. Align the other end, right side facing down, at the mark on the tote front lining. Stitch across the tab. Fold down the tab into place and topstitch across just below the fold.

Tote with pouch closure tab positioned in place for stitching

# especially for quilters

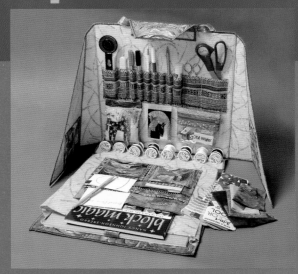

## TOOL POCKET

**1.** Fold the 20″ × 8″ piece in half lengthwise, wrong sides together, to measure 20″ × 4″ and press. The fold will be at the top of the pocket.

**2.** Stitch across the bottom of the pocket ¼″ in from the raw edges. Turn under on the stitched line and press. Topstitch in place using a ⅛″ seam.

**3. Mark the tool pocket.** Beginning at the left side of the pocket, mark a line from top to bottom ¼″ in from the left edge. Mark a parallel line 2¼″ from the first line to hold a rotary cutter. Mark the next line 1¼″ away for a ruler or gauge. Mark the next 3 lines each 1⅛″ away for markers. Mark the next 3 lines each 1″ away for pencils or chalk markers. Mark the next line 2″ away for a glue stick. Mark the next line 1¾″ away for small scissors. Mark the last line 3″ away for large scissors. (See page 21 for instructions for scissor sheaths.) Trim off the excess pocket fabric ¼″ beyond the last line. Fold under on the first and last ¼″ marks and press. (To create a pocket that accommodates your particular tools, see Custom Pockets on page 41.)

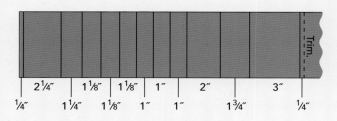

**Marked tool pocket**

**4.** **Mark the tote back.** On the tote back lining, mark a horizontal line 5¼″ down from the top. Mark a vertical line 1″ in from each raw side edge, starting ¼″ above the horizontal line and ending 4½″ below it. Measure and mark the remaining parallel lines as shown.

> **Tip**
>
> Mark your lines as thin and as accurate as possible. Even a thread width, multiplied by 10, can cause you to be off. Start on the left and work toward the right. It's okay if the last space is a bit smaller than 3″.

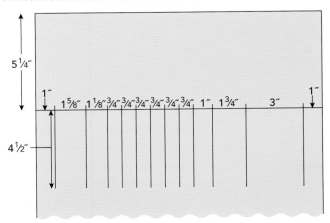

Marked tote back

**5.** **Attach the tool pocket.** Place the pocket right side up, with the left turned-under edge against the line 1″ from the tote back's left edge. Align the top edge of the pocket with the horizontal line. Stitch down the left side of the pocket ⅛″ in from the edge. Pull the pocket over to align the next line on the pocket with the next line on the tote. Stitch down the line. Secure the stitching lines with backstitching. Continue matching pocket lines to tote back lines and stitching in place, stopping before the last marked line.

**6.** Place the right folded-under edge of the pocket on the line 1″ from the tote's right side. Stitch down the right side of the pocket ⅛″ in from the edge.

**7.** Stitch across the bottom edge of the pocket, making small tucks in the bottom as needed. Start stitching *after* the division for the large scissors, leaving that division open on the bottom. The point of the large scissors will go down through this division.

> **Tip**
>
> As you sew, fold each tuck *away* from the foot and toward yourself. Just before sewing over it, use a stiletto to push the underneath side of the tuck under the foot.

**Use a stiletto to make stitching the tucks easy.**

> **Tip**
>
> Use your vinyl scraps to make a sheath for your pointed scissors. Simply fold a piece of vinyl around the closed points and mark a line along the open edge on the vinyl. Stitch on the line, rounding the bottom and backstitching at the fold. Trim the vinyl ⅛″ from the stitching.

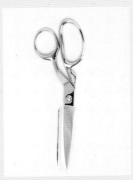

**Marking vinyl for a scissor sheath**     **Finished scissor sheath**

# PINCUSHION

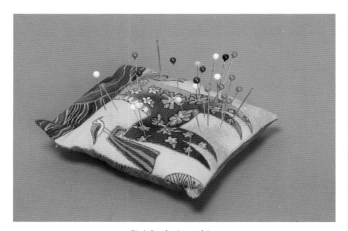

**Finished pincushion**

> **Tip**
>
> If you're fussy cutting the pincushion, you can make it any size. Cut the front ¼" beyond the area that you are featuring. Cut the back the same width as the front and the same length as the front plus 1¾". Sew the front to the back at the bottom edge of the featured area using a ¼" seam. Use the seamline as your fold line when constructing the pincushion.

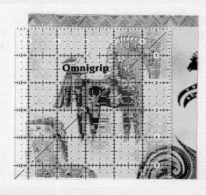

**Fussy cutting**

**1.** On the 4" × 9½" piece of fabric, press under ¼" along the 4" end that will be at the top. Measure 3½" from the turned-under edge and mark a line across the wrong side of the fabric.

**2.** Mark a line 1¼" up from the opposite edge on the right side of the fabric. Place a 3" piece of hook-and-loop tape (soft side) at the line and sew in place.

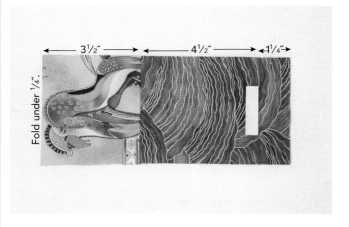

**3.** Fold on the marked lines, right sides together. The unfinished edge should lap over the turned-back edge. This will form the flap that is attached to the tote. Sew down each side with a ¼" seam allowance.

**Pincushion folded**

**4.** Clip corners and turn. Stuff it tightly with fiberfill, filling the cushion but not the flap. Topstitch across the open end. Loosely hand stitch through the center of the pincushion by making a couple of stitches and then tying off on the back to hold.

# NEEDLE CASE

**Finished needle case**

**1.** Fold the 3″ × 8¾″ needle case piece in half cross-wise to measure 3″ × 4⅜″ and press.

**2.** Sew a 2″ piece of hook-and-loop tape (soft side) just below the pressed line on the side that will become the back (attached to the tote).

**3.** With the right side up, press ¼″ under on the end of the back. Then press ¼″ under on one end of the lining piece.

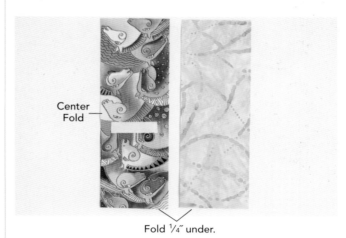

Center Fold

Fold ¼″ under.

**Pieces for the needle case**

**4.** Place the lining on the case, right sides together. Use a ¼″ seam to sew around 3 sides, leaving the end with the folded-under edges open. Clip corners and turn.

**5.** Slide a 2¼″ × 3¾″ piece of template plastic into the front (sewn) end of the needle case and baste across at the centerline.

**6.** Slide another 2¼″ × 3¾″ piece of template plastic into the back of the needle case and topstitch across the open end.

**7.** With the lining side up, place the 2″ × 7½″ felt piece on top of the needle case and stitch in place across the center. Fold the needle case closed and edgestitch across the center fold.

**Felt piece sewn into needle case**

# THREAD HOLDER

**1.** Mark evenly around the edges of the tote bottom, lining side up, to create a rectangle measuring 2¾" × 14".

**NOTE:** *The measurements given in Steps 2 and 3 are for large spools of thread. If you use smaller spools, adjust the measurements accordingly.*

**2.** Beginning in the center of the marked rectangle, mark every 1¾" in both directions, stopping before the ends.

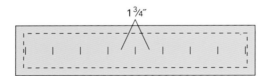

**Marked tote bottom**

**3.** Cut the elastic to 23" and mark a line ½" from one end. Mark a line every 2¾", ending about ½" from the opposite end.

**4.** Align the first mark on the elastic with the first mark at one end of the tote bottom. Stitch across the elastic, leaving the ½" end of elastic free.

**5.** Match the marks on the elastic with the marks on the tote bottom and stitch across each mark to create loops that will hold your thread spools.

**Match the marks on the tote to the marks on the elastic.**

# REMOVABLE VINYL ZIPPERED POUCH

**1.** Fold the 3" × 5½" strips of fabric in half lengthwise, wrong sides together, and press. Open with the wrong side of the fabric facing up. Fold each outside edge to the center pressed line and press. Fold at the center, wrong sides together, and press.

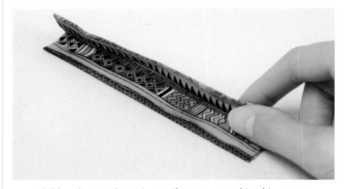

**Fold and press the strips as if you were making bias tape.**

**2.** Place the center fold of the fabric strip on top of the zipper, ⅛" from the zipper teeth. Align the end of the strip even with the upper end of the zipper tape.

Use a zipper foot to stitch along the folded edge of the fabric strip. Sew the other fabric strip to the other side of the zipper in the same manner.

**Stitch the center fold of the fabric strips to the zipper.**

**3.** The 5½″ × 3½″ piece of Quilter's Vinyl (Sources, page 47) is the front of the pouch, and the 5½″ × 5½″ piece is the back. Center a 2″ piece of hook-and-loop tape (soft side) on the back of the vinyl pouch 1″ down from the top edge and stitch it into place.

**Stitch the hook-and-loop tape onto the back piece of vinyl.**

> **Tip**
>
> Use invisible thread in the top and the bobbin

**4.** Slip the front vinyl piece between the folds of the fabric strip and stitch close to the fabric's edge. Slip the back vinyl piece into the other side of the strip and stitch close to the fabric's edge.

**Slide the vinyl between the edges of the fabric strips and stitch into place along the edge.**

**5.** With the zipper *closed,* slowly stitch back and forth across the teeth several times, ½″ up from the end of the fabric strips. Trim the zipper even with the end of the fabric strips.

**6.** With the zipper *open,* fold the right sides of the vinyl pieces together, aligning the bottom and side edges. The zipper with attached fabric strips will be on the front half. Use a ¼″ seam to stitch each side and across the bottom, backstitching at the top and corners.

> **Tip**
>
> You should be able to sew on the vinyl without making any adjustments to your machine. However, if you are having problems, try adjusting the foot pressure, using a walking foot, or using a Teflon foot.

**7.** Mark a line on each side seam ½″ above the bottom seamline and on the bottom seam ½″ in from each side seam. Align the bottom seam with the side seam and finger-press the corner flat. Stitch across at the ½″ marks. Repeat on the other corner.

**Mark the bottom corners.**     **Stitch the bottom corners.**

**8.** Trim the corners ¼″ from the stitching line. Clip the upper corners and turn. (As your hands warm the vinyl, it becomes easier to turn.) Push out the corners as much as possible.

**Tip**

A great way to soften the vinyl is to use a hair dryer. Just blow warm air on the pouch until the vinyl becomes soft and pliable.

You can also place the vinyl pouch beneath a Teflon pressing sheet. Set the iron on a medium/low setting with no steam. Hold the iron just above the pressing sheet for about 30 seconds. Turn the pouch over and repeat. Your vinyl should be soft and easy to work with until it cools.

**9.** Arrange the pincushion, needle case, and vinyl pouch on the tote back. Mark the placement positions for the hook-and-loop tape. Stitch the hook-and-loop tape (stiff side) into place on the tote back.

**10.** Refer to Preparing for Assembly and Putting It All Together (pages 42–46) to finish your tote.

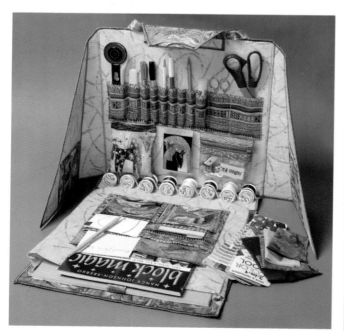

**Finished interior of the Take-It Tote for Quilters**

**Tip**

Make a design/sandpaper board to slide into the pouch so you can take it with you. Use a sharp utility knife to cut a piece of foam core board 12″ × 12″. Glue a 12″ × 12″ piece of felt (light gray is best so as not to overpower your fabric colors) on one side and a piece of very fine sandpaper on the other.

**Tip**

Slide an 11″ × 11″ June Tailor Quilter's Cut 'n Press (Sources, page 47) inside your tote. Slip the tote's top closure through the handle opening on the Cut 'n Press, and you're ready to go.

# especially for scrapbookers

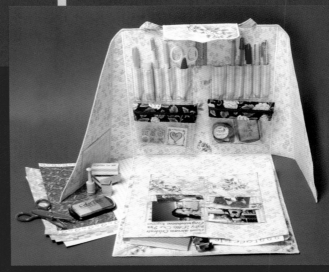

## TOOL POCKETS

**1.** Cut the 20″ × 8″ tool pocket fabric into 2 pieces, each measuring 9½″ × 8″. Fold each piece in half lengthwise, wrong sides together, to measure 9½″ × 4″. Press. The fold will be at the top of each pocket.

**2.** Stitch across the bottom of each pocket ¼″ in from the raw edges. Turn under on the sewing line and press. Topstitch in place using a ⅛″ seam.

**3. Mark the left tool pocket.** Beginning at the left side of the pocket, mark a line from top to bottom ¼″ in from the left edge. Mark a parallel line 1¼″ from the first line for a large marker. Mark the next line 2″ away for a glue stick. Mark the next 2 lines each 1⅜″ away for various markers. Mark the next line 1¾″ away for scissors. Trim off the excess pocket fabric ¼″ beyond the last line. Fold under on the first ¼″ mark and press. (To create pockets that accommodate your particular tools, see Custom Pockets on page 41.)

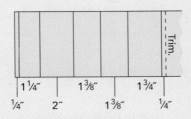

**Marked left tool pocket**

**4.** **Mark the right tool pocket.** Beginning at the left side of the pocket, mark a line from top to bottom, ¼" in from the left edge. Mark a parallel line 1¾" away for scissors. Mark the next line 1" away for a mechanical pencil. Mark the next 3 lines each 1⅛" apart for various pens and pencils. Mark the last line 1¼" away for a large marker. Trim off the excess pocket fabric ¼" beyond the last line. Fold under and press.

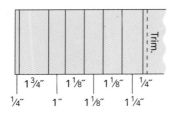

**Marked right tool pocket**

**5.** **Mark the tote back.** On the tote back lining, mark a horizontal line 5¼" down from the top. Mark parallel lines on each side 1" in from the side edges, starting ¼" above the horizontal line and ending 4½" below it. Measure and mark the remaining parallel lines as shown. You will have 12 divisions, including the center space for the ruler pocket.

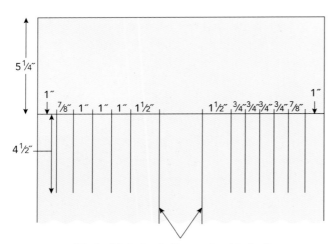

**Marked tote back, lines extend to bottom**

**6.** **Attach the left pocket.** Place the pocket right side up with the turned-under edge against the line 1" from the tote back's left edge. Align the top edge of the pocket with the horizontal line. Stitch down the left side of the pocket ⅛" in from the edge. Pull the pocket over to align the next line on the pocket with the next line on the tote. Stitch down the line. Secure the stitching lines with backstitching. Continue matching pocket lines to tote back lines and stitching in place, stopping before the last marked line. Use a basting stitch to hold the last line in place. Leave the right ¼" raw edge lying flat. It will be covered with the ruler pocket.

**7.** **Attach the right pocket.** Place the pocket right side up with the turned-under edge against the line 1" from the tote back's right edge. The top fold of the pocket should be next to the horizontal line. Topstitch down the right edge using a ⅛" seam. Pull the pocket over to match the lines and stitch in the same manner as you did for the left pocket in Step 6. The left ¼" raw edge will be covered with the ruler pocket.

**8.** Stitch across the bottom edge of the pockets, making small tucks in the bottom as needed. Stop stitching before the scissor pockets, leaving the bottom open for scissor tips to poke out if necessary. (Use a stiletto to make stitching the tucks easy. See the tip on page 21.)

## RULER POCKET

## REMOVABLE POUCHES

See the directions for making the Removable Vinyl Zippered Pouch (page 24). Make two pouches with the following changes:

- In Step 1, substitute the 3" × 5½" strips of fabric used in the Quilter's Tote with the 3" × 7" strips of fabric.

- In Step 3, substitute the 5½" × 3½" and the 5½" × 5½" pieces of vinyl used in the quilter's tote with the 7" × 4½" and the 7" × 6½" pieces of vinyl.

- In Step 7, mark the line ⅝" above the bottom seamline (instead of ½").

- Arrange the vinyl pouches on the tote back. Mark the placement positions for the hook-and-loop tape and stitch the hook-and-loop tape (stiff side) on the tote back as marked.

- Refer to Preparing for Assembly and Putting It All Together (pages 42–46) to finish your tote.

**1.** Fold the 2¾" × 20" piece in half, right sides together, to measure 2¾" × 10". Use a ¼" seam allowance to stitch each side, leaving the bottom open. Clip corners, turn, and press.

**2.** Place the ruler pocket right side up on top of the tote back lining. The edges should cover the raw edges of the tool pockets. Place the top of the ruler pocket even with the tops of the tool pockets. Topstitch the sides in place using a ⅛" seam. Backstitch to secure. Trim the bottom even with the tote bottom and stitch across the bottom ⅝" from the lower edge.

**Tip**

Use temporary spray adhesive to hold the pocket in place while stitching.

## TOOL POCKET

**1.** Fold the 8″ × 8″ piece of fabric in half, wrong sides together, and press. The folded edge will be the top of the pocket.

**2.** Stitch across the bottom of the pocket ¼″ in from the raw edges. Turn under on the sewing line and press. Topstitch in place using a ⅛″ seam.

**3.** Beginning at the left side of the pocket, mark a line from top to bottom ¼″ in from the unfinished left side. Mark a parallel line ⅞″ away from the first line for a crochet hook. Mark the next line 1″ away for a pencil. Mark the next line ¾″ away for a smaller hook. Mark the next line 1¾″ away for scissors. Mark the next line 1″ away for a marker. Mark the next line ⅞″ away for a mechanical pencil. Trim off the excess pocket fabric ¼″ beyond the last line.

**4.** Mark the back of the tote and attach this pocket when you attach the Straight Needle Pockets (page 31). (To create a pocket that accommodates your particular tools, see Custom Pockets on page 41.)

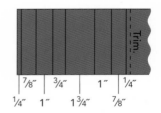

**Marked center pocket**

# STRAIGHT NEEDLE POCKETS

**1.** Fold each 6″ × 19″ piece in half, right sides together, to measure 6″ × 9½″.

**2.** Stitch across the bottom of each pocket ¼″ in from the raw edges. Turn under on the sewing line and press. Stitch into place using a ⅛″ seam.

**3.** **To mark the left needle pocket.** Beginning at the left side of the pocket, mark a line from top to bottom ¼″ in from the left edge. Mark a parallel line 1¼″ away from the first line. Mark another line 1¼″ away. These will fit size 13 needles. Mark the next 2 lines each 1″ away for size 10 or 11 needles. Trim off the excess pocket fabric ¼″ beyond the last line. Fold under on the line and press. Then fold under on the first ¼″ line on the left side of the pocket and press.

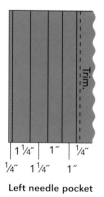

| 1¼″ | | 1″ | | ¼″ |
| --- | --- | --- | --- | --- |
| | ¼″ | | 1¼″ | 1″ |

**Left needle pocket**

**4.** **To mark the right needle pocket.** Beginning at the left side of the pocket, mark a line from top to bottom ¼″ in from the left edge. Mark a parallel line ¾″ away from the first line. Mark another line ¾″ away.

These will fit size 7 or 8 needles. Mark the next 2 lines each 1¼″ away for size 15 needles. Trim off the excess pocket fabric ¼″ beyond the last line. Fold under on the line and press. Then fold under on the first ¼″ line on the left side of the pocket and press.

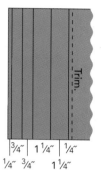

| ¾″ | | 1¼″ | | ¼″ |
| --- | --- | --- | --- | --- |
| ¼″ | ¾″ | | 1¼″ | |

**Right needle pocket**

**5.** **Mark the tote back.** On the tote back lining, mark a horizontal line 4¼″ down from the top. Mark parallel lines on each side 1″ in from the raw edges, starting ¼″ above the horizontal line and ending at the bottom edge of the tote. Measure and mark the remaining parallel lines as shown. Note that the lines for the center pocket go 4½″ below the horizontal line.

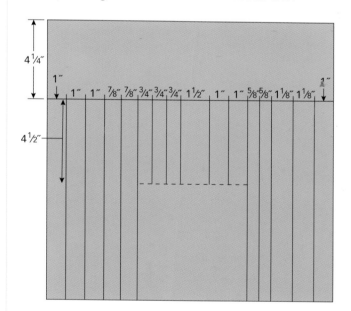

---

**Tip**

Mark your lines as thinly and as accurately as possible. Even a thread width, multiplied by 8, can cause you to be off. Start on the edges and work toward the middle. It's okay if the center space is a little bit off.

**6.** Attach the center tool pocket. Align the top of the center pocket with the horizontal line. Overlap the left unfinished edge ¼″ over the last line marked for the left needle pocket and baste down the line. Pull the pocket over to align the next line on the pocket with the next line on the tote lining and stitch down the line. Secure the stitching lines with backstitching. Continue matching pocket lines to tote back lines and stitching in place. The last line on the pocket should be on top of the first line marked for the right needle pocket. Trim the remaining pocket ¼″ from the last stitching line and baste down the line.

**7.** **Attach the left needle pocket.** Align the top edge of the pocket with the horizontal line. Line up the left edge of the left needle pocket with the line 1″ from the tote back's left edge. Stitch the pocket down the left side ⅛″ from the edge. Pull the pocket over to match the next line on the pocket with the next line on the tote lining and stitch down the line. Secure the stitching lines with backstitching and repeat across the pocket. Place the right edge on the left basted line of the center tool pocket. Stitch down the right side of the pocket ⅛″ in from the edge.

Accuracy is important to ensure that your needles will stay securely in the pockets.

**8.** **Attach the right needle pocket.** Align the top edge of the pocket with the horizontal line. Line up the right edge of the pocket with the line 1″ from the tote back's right edge. Stitch the pocket down the right side ⅛″ from the edge. Pull the pocket over to match the next line on the pocket with the next line on the tote lining and stitch down the line. Repeat across the pocket. Place the left edge of the pocket on top of the basted line on the right side of the center tool pocket. Stitch down the left side of the pocket ⅛″ in from the edge.

**9.** Stitch across the bottom edge of each pocket, making small tucks in the bottom as needed. (Use a stiletto to make stitching the tucks easy. See the tip on page 21.)

**Tip**

If your knitting needles or other accessories are too small for some of the pockets, add another line of stitching ⅛″ or more in from the original stitching lines of the pocket divisions.

## REMOVABLE POUCH

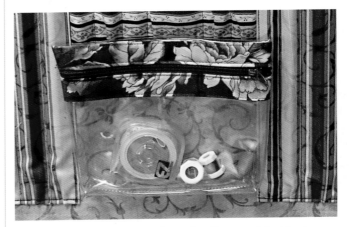

See the directions for making the Removable Vinyl Zippered Pouch (page 24). Make one pouch with the following changes:

- In Step 1, substitute the 3″ × 5½″ strips of fabric used in the Quilter's Tote with the 3″ × 7″ strips of fabric.

- In Step 3, substitute the 5½″ × 3½″ and the 5½″ × 5½″ pieces of vinyl used in the quilter's tote with the 7″ × 4½″ and the 7″ × 6½″ pieces.

- In Step 7, mark the line ⅝″ above the bottom seam-line (instead of ½″).

- Place the vinyl pouch on the tote back. Mark the placement position for the hook-and-loop tape. Stitch the hook-and-loop tape (stiff side) on the tote back as marked.

- Refer to Preparing for Assembly and Putting It All Together (pages 42–46) to finish your tote.

# especially for teachers

## Elementary School Teachers

# TOOL POCKET

**1.** Fold the 20″ × 8″ piece of fabric in half lengthwise, wrong sides together, to measure 20″ × 4″. The fold will be at the top of the pocket.

**2.** Stitch across the bottom of the pocket ¼″ in from the raw edges. Turn under on the stitching line and press. Topstitch in place using a ⅛″ seam.

**3. Mark the tool pocket.** Beginning at the left side of the pocket, mark a line from top to bottom ¼″ in from the left edge. Mark a parallel line 1¾″ away for scissors. Mark the next line 1⅝″ for a ruler. Mark the next line 2″ away for a glue stick. Mark the next line 1⅞″ away for a highlighter pen. Mark 2 more lines each 1¹⁄₁₆″ away for chalk. Mark the next 2 lines each 1″ away for pencils. Mark the next 2 lines each 1⅞″ away for dry erase markers. Mark the next 2 lines each 1⅜″ away for permanent pens. Trim off the excess pocket fabric ¼″ beyond the last line. Fold under on the line and press. Then fold under on the first ¼″ line on the left side of the pocket and press. (To create a pocket that accommodates your particular tools, see Custom Pockets on page 41.)

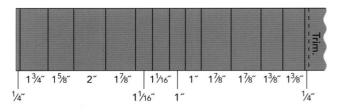

**Marked tool pocket**

**4. Mark the tote back.** On the tote back lining, mark a horizontal line 5¼″ down from the top. Mark parallel lines on each side 1″ in from the raw edges, starting each vertical line ¼″ above the horizontal line and ending 4½″ below it. Measure and mark the remaining parallel lines as shown.

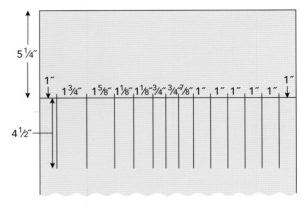

**Marked tote back**

**5. Attach the tool pocket.** Place the pocket right side up, with the left turned-under edge against the line 1″ from the tote back's left edge. Align the top edge of the pocket with the horizontal line. Stitch down the left side of the pocket ⅛″ in from the edge. Pull the pocket over to align the next line on the pocket with the next line on the tote. Stitch down the line. Secure the stitching lines with backstitching. Continue matching pocket lines to tote back lines and stitching in place, stopping before the last marked line. Place the ¼″ turned-under edge of the pocket's right side on the line 1″ from the right edge of the tote and stitch down the right side of the pocket ⅛″ in from the edge.

**6.** Stitch across the bottom edge of the pocket, stopping before the ruler division. Make small tucks in the bottom as needed. On the larger divisions, make a tuck about ½″ in from the division lines on each side. The ruler and scissor divisions are left open at the bottom. (Use a stiletto to make stitching the tucks easy. See the tip on page 21.)

**Tip**

If your markers or other items are too small for some of the pockets and slide out too easily, just add another line of stitching ⅛″ or more in from the original stitching lines of the pocket divisions.

## REMOVABLE POUCH

# Music Teachers

See the directions for making the Removable Vinyl Zippered Pouch (page 24). Make two pouches with the following changes:

- In Step 1, substitute the 3″ × 5½″ strips of fabric used in the Quilter's Tote with the 3″ × 7″ strips of fabric.

- In Step 3, substitute the 5½″ × 3½″ and the 5½″ × 5½″ pieces of vinyl used in the quilter's tote with the 7″ × 4½″ and the 7″ × 6½″ pieces of vinyl.

- In Step 7, mark the line ⅝″ above the bottom seamline (instead of ½″).

- Arrange the vinyl pouches on the tote back. Mark the placement positions for the hook-and-loop tape. Stitch the hook-and-loop tape (stiff side) on the tote back as marked.

- Refer to Preparing for Assembly and Putting It All Together (pages 42–46) to finish your tote.

# TOOL POCKET

**1.** Follow Steps 1 and 2 (page 34) of the Elementary School Teacher's Tote tool pocket to fold and stitch the pocket.

**2. Mark the tool pocket.** Beginning at the left side of the pocket, mark a line from top to bottom ¼˝ in from the left edge. Mark a parallel line 4½˝ away from the first line for a pitch pipe. Mark another line 2⅝˝ away for an electronic metronome. Mark 2 more lines each 1¹⁄₁₆˝ away for chalk. Mark the next line 1˝ away for a pencil. Mark the next 2 lines each 1⅞˝ away for dry erase markers. Mark the next 2 lines each at 1⅜˝ for permanent pens. Mark the last line ⅞˝ away for a baton. Trim off the excess pocket fabric ¼˝ beyond the last line. Fold under on the line and press. Then fold under on the first ¼˝ line on the left side of the pocket and press. (To create a pocket that accommodates your particular tools, see Custom Pockets on page 41.)

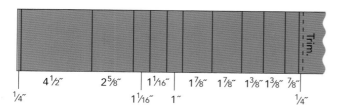

**Marked tool pocket**

**3. Mark the tote back.** On the tote back lining, mark a horizontal line 5¼˝ down from the top. Mark parallel lines on each side 1˝ in from the side edges, starting

each line ¼˝ above the horizontal line and ending 4½˝ below it. Measure and mark the remaining parallel lines as shown.

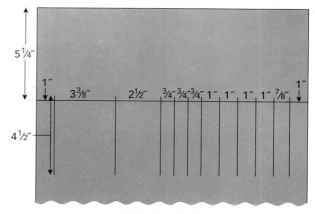

**Marked tote back**

Mark your lines as thinly and as accurately as possible. Even a thread width, multiplied by 9 can cause you to be off. Start on the right and work toward the left. It's okay if the last space is a little off.

**4.** Cut a 3˝ piece of elastic and sew it to the back side of the pocket near the top in the 4½˝ division for the pitch pipe. Begin at the line on one side of the division. Backstitch to secure one end of the elastic. Use a small zigzag stitch to stretch the elastic as you sew, ending just before the line at the end of the division. Backstitch again.

**5.** Follow Steps 5 and 6 (page 34) of the Elementary School Teacher's Tote Tool Pocket instructions to attach the pocket.

If your markers or other items are too small for some of the pockets and slide out easily, just add another line of stitching ⅛˝ or more in from the original stitching lines of the pocket divisions.

**6.** Refer to the Removable Vinyl Pouch instructions (pages 24–25) of the Elementary School Teacher's Tote to make the vinyl pouches.

**7.** Refer to Preparing for Assembly and Putting It All Together (pages 42–46) to finish your tote.

# especially for
# girls on the go

## TOOL POCKET

**1.** Fold the 20″ × 7″ piece of fabric in half lengthwise, wrong sides together, to measure 20″ × 3½″; press. The fold will be at the top of the pocket.

**2.** Stitch across the bottom of the pocket ¼″ in from the raw edges. Fold under on the stitched line and press. Topstitch in place using a ⅛″ seam.

**3. Mark the tool pocket.** Beginning at the left side of the pocket, mark a line from top to bottom ¼″ in from the left edge. Mark a parallel line 3¼″ away for a cell phone or tube of lotions. Mark another line 2¼″ away for a small MP3 player or a comb. Mark the next line 1¼″ away for a nail file. Mark the next line 3¾″ away for a compact or mirror. Mark the next line 1¾″ away for a hairbrush. Mark the next line 1⅝″ away for lipstick. Mark the next line 1¼″ away for lip gloss. Mark the next line ⅝″ away for a small brush. Mark the last line 1⅜″ away for a blush brush. Trim off the excess pocket fabric ¼″ from the last marked line. Turn under on the line and press. Then turn under on the first ¼″ line on the left side of the pocket and press. (To create a pocket that accommodates your particular tools, see Custom Pockets on page 41.)

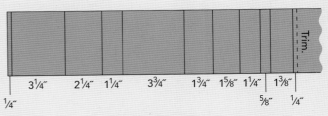

**Marked tool pocket**

**4. Mark the tote back.** On the tote back lining, mark a horizontal line 5¼" down from the top. Mark parallel lines on each side 1" in from the side edges, starting each line ¼" above the horizontal line and ending 4" below it. Measure and mark the remaining parallel lines as shown.

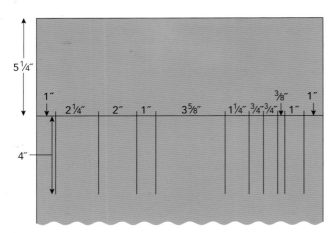

Marked tote back

**Tip**

Mark your lines as thinly and as accurately as possible. Even a thread width, multiplied by 8 can cause you to be off. Start on the edges and work toward the 2" space. It's okay if that space is a bit smaller than 2".

**5. Attach the tool pocket.** Place the pocket right side up, with the left turned-under edge against the line 1" from the tote back's left edge. Align the top edge of the pocket with the horizontal line. Stitch down the left side of the pocket ⅛" in from the edge. Pull the pocket over to align the next line on the pocket with the next line on the tote. Stitch down the line. Secure the stitching lines with backstitching. Continue matching pocket lines to tote back lines and stitching in place, stopping before the last marked line. Trim off any excess pocket fabric ¼" past the last marked line. With the turned-under edge on the pocket's right side against the line 1" from the tote's right edge, stitch down the right side of the pocket ⅛" in from the edge.

**6.** Stitch across the bottom edge of the pocket, stopping and backstitching before the hairbrush division. Make small tucks in the bottom as needed. The large divisions need 2 tucks, each placed approximately ½" in from the sewn division lines. (Use a stiletto to make stitching the tucks easy. See tip on page 21.)

**Tip**

If some of your items are too small for the pockets, just add another line of stitching ⅛" or more in from the original stitching lines of the pocket divisions. This should keep the items from slipping out of the pockets.

## REMOVABLE POUCH

See the directions for making the Removable Vinyl Zippered Pouch (page 24). Make two pouches with the following changes:

- For one of the pouches in Step 1 substitute the 3" × 5½" strips of fabric used in the Quilter's Tote with the 3" × 9" strips of fabric.

- For one of the pouches, in Step 3 substitute the 5½" × 3½" and the 5½" × 5½" pieces of vinyl used in the Quilter's Tote with the 9" × 4½" and the 9" × 6½" pieces of vinyl.

- In Step 7, mark the line ⅝" above the bottom seam-line (instead of ½").

- Arrange the vinyl pouches on the tote back. Mark the placement positions for the hook-and-loop tape. Stitch the hook-and-loop tape (stiff side) on the tote back as marked.

- Refer to Preparing for Assembly and Putting It All Together (pages 42–46) to finish your tote.

# especially for
# kids on the go

## TOOL POCKET

**1.** Fold the 20″ × 8″ piece of fabric in half lengthwise, wrong sides together, to measure 20″ × 4″. Press. The fold will be at the top of the pocket.

**2.** Stitch across the bottom of the pocket ¼″ in from the raw edges. Turn under on the sewing line and press. Topstitch in place using a ⅛″ seam.

**3. Mark the tool pocket.** Beginning at the left side of the pocket, mark a line from top to bottom ¼″ in from the left edge. Mark a parallel line 1⅝″ away. Mark the next 5 lines each 1½″ apart. These 6 divisions will be for washable markers. Mark the next line 1¹⁄₁₆″ away for chalk. Mark the next line 1″ away for a pencil. Mark the next line 2″ away for scissors. Mark the next line 6″ away for a box of flashcards, an electronic game, or another item of your choice. Trim off the excess pocket fabric ¼″ from the last marked line. Turn under on the line and press. Then turn under on the first ¼″ line on the pocket's left side and press. (To create a pocket that accommodates your particular tools, see Custom Pockets on page 21.)

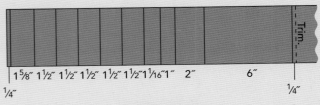

¼″ 1⅝″ 1½″ 1½″ 1½″ 1½″ 1½″ 1¹⁄₁₆″ 1″ 2″ 6″ Trim. ¼″

**Marked tool pocket**

**4.** Cut a 4″ piece of elastic and sew it to the back side of the pocket near the top in the 6″ division. Begin at the line on one side of the division. Backstitch to secure one end of the elastic. Use a small zigzag stitch to stretch the elastic as you sew, ending just before the line at the end of the division. Backstitch again.

**5. Mark the tote back.** On the lining side of the tote back, mark a horizontal line 5¼″ down from the top. Mark parallel lines on each side 1″ in from the side edges, starting each line ¼″ above the horizontal line and ending 4½″ below it. Measure and mark the remaining parallel lines as shown.

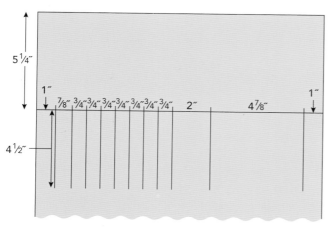

Marked tote back

### Tip

Mark your lines as thinly and as accurately as possible. Even a thread width, multiplied by 9, can cause you to be off. Start on the left and work toward the right. It's okay if the 6″ space is a bit off.

**6. Attach the tool pocket.** Place the pocket right side up, with the left turned-under edge against the line 1″ from the tote back's left edge. Align the top edge of the pocket with the horizontal line. Stitch down the left side of the pocket ⅛″ in from the edge. Pull the pocket over to align the next line on the pocket with the next line on the tote. Stitch down the line. Secure the stitching lines with backstitching. Continue matching pocket lines to tote back lines and stitching in place, stopping before the last marked line. With the folded edge on

top of the line 1″ from the tote's right edge, backstitch down the side of the pocket ⅛″ in from the edge.

**7.** Stitch along the bottom edge of the tool pocket, making tucks as needed. On the large divisions, make 2 tucks, each placed about ½″ in from the division lines. (Use a stiletto to make stitching the tucks easy. See the tip on page 21.)

## REMOVABLE POUCH

See the directions for making the Removable Vinyl Zippered Pouch (page 24). Make two pouches with the following changes:

- In Step 1, substitute the 3″ × 5½″ strip of fabric used in the Quilter's Tote with the 3″ × 7″ strip of fabric.

- In Step 3, substitute the 5½″ × 3½″ and the 5½″ × 5½″ pieces of vinyl used in the Quilter's Tote with the 7″ × 4½″ and the 7″ × 6½″ pieces of vinyl.

- In Step 7, mark the line ⅝″ above the bottom seam-line (instead of ½″).

- Arrange the vinyl pouches on the tote back. Mark the placement positions for the hook-and-loop tape. Stitch the hook-and-loop tape (stiff side) on the tote back as marked.

# CUSTOM POCKETS

The fabric for the custom tool pocket is cut 20″ wide and 8″ long. The pockets are folded in half across the width of the fabric to make a piece that is 20″ × 4″. The fold will always be placed at the top of the pocket. When you cut the pockets, place the fabric so the pattern on the front of the pocket is going in the right direction.

1. Cut the tool pocket 20″ × 8″. Fold in half lengthwise, wrong sides together, to measure 20″ × 4″. Press. The fold will be at the top.

2. Stitch across the bottom of the pocket ¼″ in from the raw edges. Turn under on the stitched line and press. Topstitch in place using a ⅛″ seam.

3. **Mark the tool pocket.** Begin at the left side of the pocket and mark a line from top to bottom ¼″ in from the left edge. Fold under on the line and press.

4. **Mark the tote back.** With lining side up, mark the tool pocket's placement across the tote back with a horizontal line 5¼″ down from the top. Mark parallel lines on each side 1″ in from the side edges, starting ¼″ above the line marked across the top and ending 4½″ below it.

5. **Attach the pocket.** Place the pocket right side up, with the turned-under edge against the 1″ line marked on the tote back's left side. The top fold of the pocket should be next to the line marked across the top. Stitch down the left side of the pocket ⅛″ in from the edge.

6. **Custom fit the item.** Place the item that you are custom fitting onto the tote back next to the line you just stitched. Place the pocket on top of the item and pull the pocket over it. Place a ruler over the pocket at the item's open side, pushing the ruler snugly against the item. Mark the pocket. Before releasing the ruler, mark the tote back ¼″ above and below the pocket.

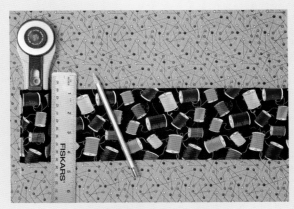

**Customizing your tool pocket**

7. Remove the item. Make sure your lines are straight, even if your item is not. Keeping the pocket line even with the marks on the tote back, stitch down the line, backstitching at the top and bottom. If you are making several divisions of the same size, mark them all before stitching. If your items slide out of the pockets too easily, just add another line of stitching ⅛″ inside the divisions.

8. If you are making a pocket for a particularly large item, add an elastic strip to keep the item securely in the pocket. (See Step 4 for the pitch pipe pocket on page 36.)

9. Before stitching the last division, trim off excess pocket fabric ¼″ beyond the last division line. Turn under and finger press before stitching.

10. Stitch across the bottom edge of the pocket, making small tucks in the bottom as needed. (Use a stiletto to make stitching the tucks easy. See the tip on page 21.)

11. Refer to Preparing for Assembly and Putting It All Together (pages 42–46) to finish your tote.

# preparing for
# assembly

## FUSING THE EXTERIOR

1. **If using fast2fuse, go to Step 2.** Center the pieces of fusible on each piece of the tote, stabilizer side up.

2. Fuse the outside fabric to all pieces of the tote.

## TRIMMING

1. Trim the front and back pieces of the tote to 14″ × 14″. Trim off the excess from the edges evenly around all sides to be sure the fabric and stabilizer are secure on the trimmed edges.

2. Trim the bottom to 2¾″ × 14″.

3. Cut one of each side and flap (see pages 12–13) with the pattern facing up, and one of each with the pattern facing down. Trim the flaps, the top closure (page 14), and the sides according to the pattern pieces, making sure to use the lines marked for trimming. (Save all the scraps to test your satin stitching!

**Tip**

Spray the pattern pieces with temporary adhesive spray to hold them in place while cutting.

4. Cut the top closure at the 1″ intervals, according to Pattern Piece 2 (page 14).

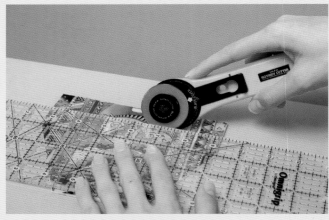

**Cutting the top closure**

**Place the hook-and-loop tape on the front.**

> **Tip**
>
> Personalize the tote by embroidering your name (or the name of the lucky recipient) on the inside of the 1″ piece that will be on the inside of the tote.

**Embroider your name inside the top closure.**

# HOOK-AND-LOOP TAPE

**1.** On the bottom of the tote front, measure ¼″ up from the edge at the center and mark a short line. Center a 1½″ × ¾″ piece of hook-and-loop tape (soft side) above the line on the tote front. Pin the pouch to the inside of the tote so it is out of the way. Stitch the hook-and-loop tape into place.

**2.** Sew a 1½″ piece of hook-and-loop tape (soft side) to the outside of the tote front 1¼″ down from the center top edge. Pin the pouch pocket and closure tab out of the way on the lining side so you don't catch them in the stitching.

**3.** Place a 2″ piece of hook-and-loop tape (soft side) on the outside of the right front flap, beginning at the tip of the flap ¼″ up from the lower edge. Trim the hook-and-loop tape to fit the point. Stitch into place. There should be a piece of hook-and-loop tape on the inside of the flap directly beneath the piece you are stitching.

**Place the hook-and-loop tape on the flap.**

# putting it all
# together

## Get Ready for Stitching

**1.** I prefer a topstitch needle for stitching. If you have a built-in walking foot, disengage it for this process. Set the satin stitch width at 4.5 and the length at 0.4. Loosen your upper tension to about 3 or to the tension necessary for a nice stitch.

> **Tip**
> Machine embroidery thread gives the stitching a pretty sheen.

**2.** Use the narrow-edge foot to test the stitching on some of the scraps left over from trimming the sides. Butt 2 pieces together and stitch, being sure to center the stitching over both edges. Your pieces should feed evenly without pushing. If you are not having success with the suggested settings, try other settings until you get the proper result. Your stitches should give fairly good, but not complete, coverage, and your piece should feed evenly without pushing it through.

**3.** For the second stitching, change the stitch width to 6 and the length to 0.3. Switch to an open-toe or appliqué foot. Practice stitching over the first line, centering the second line of stitching over the first. After the second stitching, you should have good coverage.

> **Tip**
> If you are experiencing thread breakage, try a different kind of thread, as some machines just don't like some threads.

## STITCH THE PIECES

**1.** Use the proper settings on your machine and the narrow-edge foot to attach the sides to the back of the tote, butting the pieces together. Change the stitch length and width and then switch to an open-toe or appliqué foot for the second stitching. Attach all pieces (according to the steps below), using this same stitching order. After the second stitching, always check to make sure you have complete coverage on the back and the front. Occasionally, a third stitching is necessary.

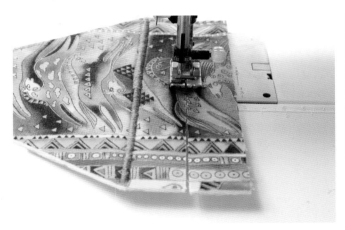

Stitch the pieces together using the narrow-edge foot.

Switch to an open-toe foot for the second stitching.

2. Attach the front flaps to the sides.

3. Attach the bottom of the tote to the back.

4. Attach the front of the tote to the bottom.

5. Stitch along all remaining outside edges. Use the open-toe or appliqué foot and set the satin stitch width and length so that it is the same as for the first stitching (Step 1). Stitch along the top edge of the tote back, moving across the sides and down the front flaps. As you stitch the edges, try to let the needle fall just over the outside edge or, if using cording, over the cording. Set the stitch width and length to the setting for the second stitching and stitch again. At the outside corners, continue the stitching to the very edge before the turn. Turn the corner and take a few stitches forward. Then backstitch to the very edge before going forward. Be sure to lock your stitches when starting and stopping.

## OPTIONAL CORDING

Thanks to Linda Johansen and her book *Fast, Fun & Easy Fabric Boxes* (see Sources, page 47), I learned how to use cording around the outside edges of the totes to strengthen them. This is optional. If you decide to use cording, you will need about 4 1/2 yards of 1/16" polyester cording or size 3 Fashion Crochet Thread by Coats & Clark. Hold the cord next to the tote's outside edges as you stitch your first line of edgestitching, keeping slight pressure on the cord as you stitch. Again, practice on some scraps first. Your needle should fall just beyond the outside edge of the cord and should catch the edge of the tote on the other side. Clip the ends of the cording as close as possible and treat them with seam sealant.

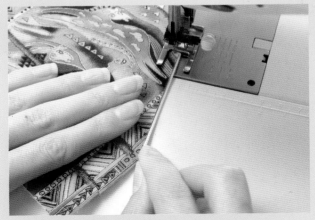

Pull the cording slightly to keep it next to the edge.

6. Attach the top closure tab to the 1" pieces that were cut from it, as in Step 2.

7. Stitch around the outside edges of the closure unit, as in Step 5.

**8.** With the tote open and the lining side up, center the top closure unit on the back of the tote at the top edge. The bottom 1″ segment of the closure should overlap the tote, so that the line of stitching attaching the segment to the closure is on top of the edgestitching on the tote back. Use a straight stitch to stitch along the lower edge of the satin stitching. Be sure to secure the stitching at both ends with backstitching.

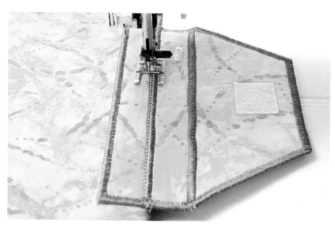

Stitch the top closure to the inside back of the tote.

## THE HANDLE

**1.** Place the 2¼″ × 25″ piece for the handle wrong side up. Turn up ¼″ on each long side and press. If you are making the Kids-on-the-Go Tote, you may want to shorten the handle by 4″ or 5″. If you are making the Girls-on-the-Go Tote, use the 2¼″ × 36″ piece for the handle.

Handle with batting inserted

**2.** Slip the ¾″ batting strip under one folded edge. Turn the opposite edge over the top to meet at the side and press. Edgestitch along the length on both sides.

Fold one side of the handle over the batting and edgestitch each side.

**3.** Form a circle with the handle. Zigzag stitch the ends together. Reinforce the stitching by stitching back and forth a few times. Place the handle with the raw edges at the center underneath the top of the closure. Secure the handle in place by stitching across each end of the top closure 3 or 4 times to reinforce the stitches.

Attach the handle to the under side of the top closure.

You've done it! Now go load your tote and hit the road. I hope it's been fun.

- **Andover Fabrics**
1384 Broadway, Suite 1500
New York, NY 10018
(800) 223-5678
www.andoverfabrics.com

- **Clothworks Textiles**
6250 Stanley Avenue South
Seattle, WA 98108
(800) 874-0541
www.clothworkstextiles.com

- **Coats & Clark—Fashion Crochet Thread**
Consumer Services
P.O. Box 12229
Greenville, SC 29612-0229
(800) 648-1479
www.coatsandclark.com

- **Collins—Sewing and Quilting Notions**
950 Brisack Road
Spartansburg, SC 29304

- **EZ Quilting by Wrights—Sewing and Quilting Notions**
P.O. Box 398
West Warren, MA 01092
(877) 597-4448
www.ezquilt.com

- **fast2fuse Double-Sided Fusible Stiff Interfacing**
  - *Fast, Fun & Easy Fabric Boxes*
  by Linda Johansen
- **Quilter's Vinyl**
C&T Publishing
P.O Box 1456
Lafayette, CA 94549
(800) 284-1114
www.ctpub.com

- **June Tailor—Quilter's Cut 'n Press**
P.O. Box 208
Richfield, WI 53076
(800) 844-5400
www.junetailor.com

- **Kandi Corp—Embellishments**
P.O. Box 8345
Clearwater, FL 33758
(800) 985–2634
www.kandicorp.com

- **Lion Brand Yarn**
135 Kero Road
Carlstadt, NJ 07072
(800) 258-YARN (9276)
www.lionbrand.com

- **Michael Miller Fabrics**
118 West 22nd Street, 5th Floor
New York, NY 10011
(212) 704-0774
www.michaelmillerfabrics.com

- **P&B Textiles**
1580 Gilbreth Road
Burlingame, CA 94010
(650) 692-0422
www.pbtex.com

- **Pellon—Craft Fuse and Decor-Bond**
4720A Stone Drive
Tucker, GA 30084
(770) 491-8001 x2980
www.shoppellon.com

- **Timeless Treasures Fabrics**
483 Broadway
New York, NY 10013
(212) 226-1400
www.ttfabrics.com

- **2 Point Media**
950 Los Osos Valley Road, Suite A-1
Los Osos, CA 93402
(805) 540-5050
www.2pointmedia.com

- **Wrights Sewing Products**
P. O. Box 398
West Warren, MA 01092
(877) 597-4448

- **YLI Corporation**
1439 Dave Lyle Boulevard #16C
Rock Hill, SC 29730
(803) 985-3100
www.ylicorp.com

*For a list of other fine books from C&T Publishing, ask for a free catalog:*

**C&T Publishing, Inc.**
P.O. Box 1456
Lafayette, CA 94549
(800) 284-1114
ctinfo@ctpub.com
www.ctpub.com

For quilting supplies:
**Cotton Patch**
1025 Brown Avenue
Lafayette, CA 94549
(800) 835-4418 or
(925) 283-7883
Email: CottonPa@aol.com
Website: www.quiltusa.com

*Fabrics used in the quilts shown may not be currently available, as fabric manufacturers keep most fabrics in print for only a short time.*

*C&T Publishing's professional photography services are now available to the public. Visit us at www.ctmediaservices.com.*

# about the author

Marilynn began sewing at age five. Before starting her career in real estate, she made most of her own clothing, as well as the clothes for her two daughters. Since retiring, she has relished having the time to delve into the quilting world, taking as many classes as possible and trying just about every new technique available.

Wearable art garments, bags, and especially quilts are among Marilynn's favorite things to create. She loves to plan a quilt from her own stash. She taught her granddaughter to sew at age five, and they have had great fun making four quilts together—so far. Marilynn has a knack for figuring out how to make things an easier way, and once she gets an idea, there's no stopping her. She says that the answers to her dilemmas usually come to her around 4 o'clock in the morning, when she'll jump out of bed and head to the sewing machine to see if the idea really works.

She and her husband, Richard, live on an acreage located between Springfield and Branson, Missouri, where they enjoy the beauty of the hills and trees of the Ozarks. A self-described "terribly addicted fabri-holic," she and Richard love to travel, especially if there are quilt shops along the way.

# Great Titles
## from C&T PUBLISHING

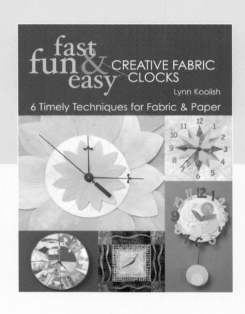

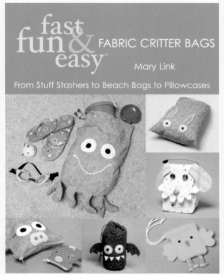
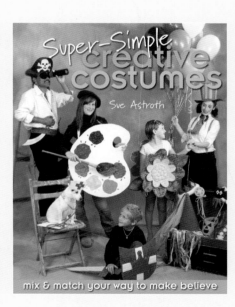